Love and Revolution

Our Love…

Our Revolution…

Jah's Creation

Love and Revolution

Sahara Wisdom aka Jah's Creation

Book Cover designed by April Blount

Published Independently in the USA
By April Blount
www.lulu.com/jahs_creation

ISBN: 978-0-578-02364-9

Contents

4

Letter from Sahara Wisdom-

They say Love and Revolution do not mix. In my experience they not only mix they collide into a magnificent starburst whenever possible. This is the premise of my book you are now holding. I want to illustrate how one cannot exist without the other.

Where there is Revolution you will find Love abounds. It can be seen in the love for our leaders who fight for our existence. You will see the Love shown as the Speaker so eloquently states the need for Justice and equality for all our People.

In these pages you will see love for the Souljah. Come experience the need for a woman to understand and take the risk of loving the man who gets paid by people who would rather see him hung by a tree. You will see unconditional love spill off these pages onto your mental plate to feast upon.

Some of the pieces will evoke love for your mate unimaginable. Others may offend you to write me and tell me so. I accept it all. I want to be proven wrong when I say we have failed in the 20th Century to find liberation.

So, my reader I humbly submit my Love for our Revolution within these pages. My hope is at least ONE piece will stick in your mind for you to ponder over. Until my pen meets paper again thank you for riding this journey with me.

2017 Note- I am now wiser in my writings, but still hold this book dear to my heart. It shows where I have been. Keep an eye out for my new children's book series.

Love

I Love To Sit Back
Watching Ur Inner-Light Shine
See Those Flock to U

They Glimpse What I See
The Ancestor's Creation
Ur Words Strong and True

Let Me Drink of U
Sip of Ur Knowledge-Wisdom
U My Perfect Verse

"Perfect Verse"
By Jah's Creation

Unconditional Love

*Loving yourself must come
before loving others!*

Too many times I have expressed this…But, never to you….

Unconditionally, you're the ONE God had to make perfect for me

From your mind to your toe nails I am in AWE of what U have become!

To touch you is to know the Ancestors' blessings

Too whisper in your mind Confidence is my sole occupation

No one will ever say these things to you and mean it- not like I do...

I love your Righteous Knowledge YOU exude despite opposition

YOU forever walk away Unscathed and Untainted... Remarkable

How did you get this way... But in your eyes I see the trail

No one knows why your lips speak what your heart reveals

Your mind embedded with truths to intercept the lies of this world

And all this being told from me to YOU...

No one can love you Jahs... Not like I do!

Bound To U-

Filled with the knowledge of Ancestors I bow 2 you
Most call me backwards or just plain wrong
But, my Third Eye sees the God in you

I don't mean to sound like a proverbial cliché'
You were fashioned for me from the top of your head
To the soles of your feet God made all you as a gift

How your essence makes me high
Each time that you are around me
Like Eve tempted at your Apple's tree

I am in awe of the DARK in you...
Held speechless by the Light in you
Paralyzed I catch the hint of your speech

Educate me Tempt me Tease me
Make me righteous
While playing unrighteous games

Bathe me in your pattern of linguistic ability
From my ears to below my navel
Cleanse me with all of you

Wanting to feel, touch, and be absorbed
By your presence, your eternal essence
The way you teach me your love lessons

Let me taste from your Banana Tree
Seeking soul satisfying nourishment
While you sip from my Honey's Dew

Loving you is like a desire King
Where we stand on the corner of passion and romance
Knowing love is only lusts desire

Standing yet not touching... seeing the line...
And barely trying to cross it... knowing what can happen

8

Will shatter atoms and make the earth's soul shake

My words are starting to run small
The mere thought of you exhausts my all
I can't keep up almost out breathe

Trying to describe my loyalty to u
Why I am bound
To your love.[1]

Eternal Loyalty

I wrote of you before your existence was a presence in my mind's eye...

I loved you even when your unclear spirit cast a shadow over my Divine light for you... Now, after vows of loving you no more I see it was a lie...

I did not walk away, but sat still and breathed in your pleas to be patient...

Patient, with a heart stronger than my own; yet catching up with what was already known; our paths meant to form Completion

Waiting for you to turn around and realize I was to be your Yoruba Destiny one of your Eternal Queens...

How many times must I endure the agonizing pull of the strings on my soul? Forevermore our Ancestors answer

Wake up in knowledge our revolution is reborn yet again Refusing failure this lifetime

Realizing it is no longer a matter of you and me. We hold an inner being- half you half me to create Eternity.

Bigger than the life inside us we continue to journey down the Road Less Traveled together.

Determined now more than ever to seek Isis' lips. Drink of her words of Enlightenment for our Union.

Seek Osiris' Supreme Knowledge. Drench our intellect in the wisdom in which he speaks.

Cast away the mere fleshly memories of our initial reactions to our mind blowing' hip actions.

Understanding the bliss of our love making is nothing in the light of the pleasures of our Awakenings of Self.

Wrap yourself in the knowledge, as you ebb and flow between me and uncertainty, my loyalty is a forever constant in this reality.

U Called Me Pretty

With one word U revealed who I was.
Through Mist of Mind U saw me come through the darkness...

Held my hand yet always keeping the sacred secret of my Conception...
U knew I was the Light that shines into our Eternity...

I had to see for myself yet the touch and lies of others had made me too blind to see...
No longer being able to hold in your knowledge of my being you called me. Pretty...

Translated into the ancient Cuneiform of Majestic...
Transcended time to Hieroglyphic Beauty...
Beyond Isis' lips and soothsayers to Enlightened Being...
To Yoruba Queen... Pretty...

My intellect remembered Babylon Mystery...
Translating the universal language of Truth...
Melded with the Language of the Birds Righteous...
Lions' roar to His Lioness Pretty...

My hair transformed from Mayan temple wisps to locks of black and white...
Stories entangled in my tresses of our past civilizations... Pretty...

My short skirt and tight shirt melting away...
Replaced with the bustier of wisdom encasing my bosom and heart...

The chalice of my womb regaled with the 7 skirts of the seas... Beautiful Oceans blue...
Pretty...
Parrot feathers flowing through my locks as I walk the path

Untouched...

Unscathed...

Pretty...

Ancient Devotions

My love is void of words spinning devotional tales and love affairs. Yet, I see the notes playing around us.

From low baritones when the world throws us strife and we pray to Eshu[2] for the protection of our home.

The light sopranos right before the orgasmic waves of Yemaya's[2] ocean deep inside me crash onto the shores of your love.

Listening to the tribal drums of *"Make his HOUSE our HOME..."* is the only call I can answer. Bowing to the force of why I was created in this walking vessel.

Inhale the cosmic melody of comforting your spirit in Oshun's[2] cooling waters. Shut your eyes heeding the sounds of streams rippling past the rocks by the rivers shores. Allow these flows to bear your fears and defeats to the farthest reaches of reality.

I see the Sea of White and Gold. The perfect revelation of our Commitment transformed. Sharing vows set in our fate since before dawn. Finally, we surrender to the love for our people to Raise up Eternity together.

The final pieces of your Collective Family intertwined in Righteousness. Place your emblem of loyalty on my right hand. As the Prophets stand at the right hand of God I will journey on the RIGHT side of *Truth*.

Our altar, the ancient formation of nature before us. Our wedding waltz the breeze rustling through majestic Ancestral Groves.

Finally, feeling the earth beneath our exposed feet- sharing our completion with family and friends.

I am Not *IN* Love

I love him- this is a fact undeniable by all who know and see me.

Yet, I refuse to fall in love.

See, I don't need bells and whistles and for the stars to align.

I refuse to melt because I hear fireworks going off. That is not love- that is the lie

My serotonin levels in my brain will not rule my intellect to fall for just anything

I am not an animal- so keep your verses of MY completion in your being

He who holds the key to my creation made me complete well before existence

So, don't get upset when I don't fall for your sexual stimulating persistence

I call you Daddy as a term of endearment to recognize your daughter MOON is your center

Not because I need one or didn't have one growing up- remember this before you enter

Yeah, that love poetry makes a part of my anatomy want to move intrinsically with your hips

But, don't get it twisted you won't catch me sending 11 messages to your one- not from these lips

There is a fine line between Needy and Loyalty- it pains me to see my sisters fall so hard

Allowing men they don't know to fill a hole no one can letting down there sacred guard

He is not my self-esteem and I do not want to be his everything in life

I can't blur the line between lover and stalker that only causes internal strife

"Why you haven't you called me?" and "I sent you messages but you didn't answer"

That erratic diatribe will eat a man's sanity away like terminally ill cancer

Searching for something only GOD can give looking for DIVINITY in earthly form

I see the GOD in you but you are not My GOD- that only causes a storm

I love him more than he will ever know and he stays with me for only one good reason

He knows I am not a child looking for a Daddy nor am I here just for a season.

And I swear this been on my mind al day must have been intervention from above...

To remind me I have a better blessing in my senses- than just merely falling in love

I Got Verses for You

Yeah, I got verses for you...
But, you have made me speechless... this poetess is at a Supreme loss...

I start with... You are you... and... The images are too bright for Man's mere words...
Strength...

Then a side of syllables missing contractions to explain the awesome power in you...

But, I swear I got verses for you King...

The Supreme Wisdom I have found... I promise it is sublime in its simplicity to stand
erect... I forget... but I swear I see...

The consonants running around in my cerebrum trying to wrap around periods...

Commas and exclamations... to Exclaim the... something that keeps me tied to you...

No wait... I KNOW I got verses for you Beloved...

The promise of a child from a Divine seed... a cry maybe a tear or two...

The frustration of not understanding why some call me a fool for you...

How can all my education seem miss-fed from my mind to my lips...

Vocals inept to form the articulated tongue to rain blessings on your head...

All this being said...Yeah I got verses for you....

Ménage a Trois

Your wife is the Music. How it dances for you.
Your teasing and giving of your ebb and flow.

You are exhibitionists to the crowd
making' every pair of hips groove with desire.

Men wishing the crowd gave it up
so easily to their vibe.

They just don't see the pain and trust built
through time and space.

Perfecting your lover's touch
making her feel your passions

Conveying your deepest desires for Revolution
to the entranced masses before you.

I sit in the back...

Watching their envy to belong to your
musical love affair.

I sway in the shadows--
A voyeur to your passions.
Understanding I am a mere mistress
Oh, how she satisfies your soul

As you step off the stage kissing me I can still
feel the vibes from your Wheels of Steel.

You want so much for your ultimate
fantasy to come true.

For me to take her in my hands. Caress her...
Letting my flow fall all over her wanting lips.

16

You see my stage fright taking my hands in
yours whispers of trust and devotion.

You have taught me what she likes...
Needing my words to become orgasmic
melodies to the waiting crowd.

Your perfect union...
Your Ménage Trois fantasy...

The D.J....

The Sound...

My Voice...

Let Me

Let Me...
Absorb the pain and confusion to give your piece-
PEACE... because baby, I love you

Quite simply I want to take in the sorrow
so all you write is joyous creations

Will you...
Let Me...

Infuse poetic lullabies and hopes
unimaginable into your Quill.

Bleed for you and use my essence
to keep your pen Righteous

Don't Deny Me...
Let Me...

Sit as your mental collides with the verses
in your soul to write Stoetries untold

Watch in awe as New Scriptures form
from you for our Revolution to live by

King Please...
Let Me...

Divine with the Cowries to ask for blessings
and make Sacrifice for your spirit

Assist in preparing the Lyrical Spiritual Wash
you allow to flow from your Ancient lips

Yes...
Let Me...

Love you beyond Spiritual or mere Flesh
for the primordial Light source in you to shine for me

Show I know I can only share you with the rest
of Humanity but knowing you own a piece of my soul
Let Me... Be that Wombman

Angry Black Wombman

Until we find love for SELF and forgiveness
for our past choices- How can we truly allow
another one of God's creatures to love us?

Your beauty is tainted by the scars you refuse to let heal...

Your don't mess with me attitude ensures...
yes your KING will do as you ask...
pass you by...and not...
mess with ...
you...

You pray to your sisters
a "good" man comes around,
and the next breathe,
no man is any good...

You step on stage and pay lip service
to the Black man to go home and bed
whatever comes to lie beside you...?

All because you "grown" and can...

Angry Black Woman...
My beautiful sister Queen-

Your beauty is tainted by the scars you refuse to let heal...

Soothing a Warrior's Spirit

When you come home saying, "Baby you won't believe..." and, "Baby they tried..."

As I slip off my dress.

And, "Can you see them trying' to take it all away?"

You look up and see the Queen before you bowing in your glory.

Can you feel the day melt away?

Allow me to undress the revolution from around you clothing you in my warmth. Let me iron the wrinkles of time and defeat from your brow.

Washing your feet in the tears of my flesh is my ultimate joy.
Lay down with me feeling the nature in me speak truth righteously to your heart.

Kiss... BENEATH me and drink the elixir that has sustained generations. Delve into my knowledge learning of the love and devotion only I can teach.

Adorning your body with the pure essence of me- from your toes to your precious locks with the respect and loyalty you deserve from your Adam's rib.

My lips kissing you making your seed flow through me to conceive our Truth- Nurture Revolution- giving birth to our future.

As the sun sets on one more day in this jungle let out your Lion's roar as our bodies intertwine into a righteous orgasmic mix of love, desire and loyalty.

Allow me to maintain this Warrior's Spirit!

Come home to me and let me soothe you into the accomplishments of your strength. Toiling 10 hours for someone who would rather hang you by a tree than sign your paycheck.

You are righteous and your home needs to be your throne to steady your pure Warrior's Spirit.

Come partake of the freshness of your fruits and rest your body with the nourishment of your family surrounding you. Eat and be full of the laughter and giggles only a baby's smile can give.

See our family colors of Mahogany Brown to shades of the Unique Essence of Eboni flourishing under our love.

Let go of the days troubles as we watch our Lost tribe of Shabazz grow strong and powerful...

Under your

Warriors

Spirit...

This... Is Love

In the morning I set out his garments-
colors matching my own made for me at his request...

I collect Aloe as I move to the sway
of his voice while he prays over herbs
meant to Wash and Heal those in need...

As Shango calls and Oya moves
right before a cleansing rain-
we dance in the grass surrounded
by Ancestral Drums

On picnics we stroll barefoot
underneath the trees allowing Oshun's
cooling waters to tickle our toes
by Her shores

Cause- see This... Is Love

Not often will these times take place
but when they do... time leaves
all transgressions and tears in faded pasts...

Until all I can remember is the last time –
the last hour-
the last moment Love came
home for a moment to just BE

See, I had past lives on this earth before him
and they all taught me what
LOVE IS NOT...

The calls wondering where he is-
or the "It's not me it is you..."
Yes I said that right...
the permanent scar in my head for
not being woman enough –
or him not Man enough to walk away...

   Yeah, I know what love AIN'T!!!

So, when Righteous Love
comes home and we talk
of the lessons we have learned-
I sit attentive to this Teacher

Lighting candles and teaching him
How they burn-
exchanging Ancient Secrets
revealed in our Visions

Twisting locs and being careful
not to hold on too tight-
For he needs to be free-
Yea, even from me

See, What I have for this Divine seed
planted and tended by the Egun* for me...

Yea- This... Is Love

*Egun- Yoruba for Ancestors

Revolution

spill your soul in ink

lyrical grace redefined

I cannot judge you

"Jah's Creation"

Haiku by Perditions Love Child[3]

Wake The Funk Up!

Wake the funk up while you waiting'
for renewed government handouts.
Wake the funk up while you chanting'
for the ones who feed you crumbs and blind the truth.

You still a nicca in their eyes they just pat you on the head and say go fetch...
Fetch this easy section 8 to keep you away from the River Oaks gates..
Fetch this slave mentality food stamp card
Go kill your selves on cheap pork and lard...
Fetch these crumbs while we eat like royalty...
Your rims may bling... But that's what they want...
Bling till you can't see truth... Spin till you dazed and confused
In so much mess you don't know you being buried in government filth.

U still a nicca in the good Dems eyes...
They still white and talk like snakes...
Thinking they our savior is a dead man's mistake...
Heed my words or see where they lead you..
We still savage to them practicing so called voodoo...
These are the same ones that made you only a third of a whole man.
They greatest pleasure is feeding you from their hand...

Do for self or get out the way.
They will hang you at the first light of day...
They will do it slow through public assistance...
Give you just enough to keep you warped in another existence.

All of them vacation in the same places...
Under different games but still the same white faces...
Blow you away not leaving any traces...
Mind gone dancing a jig in mindless mazes...

Got you dancing and praying and thanking the lord....
Calling on Jesus but still playing the white governments' whore!
You think they give a care about your kids??
They rape our history and put your seed on meds...
Something' has to be wrong with a negra child who got open eyes...
Restless because the spoiled educational food is only riddled with lies...

Like a Pac-man game we try to run from the BEAST
But in the end game you the ghost
-the sacrifice..
At this white bred...
FEAST

Stolen Truth-
Collaboration with Poet Defiant Sun

I am the truth hidden within your fallacies
The lies spoken when the truth was not worth speaking of
Still they whispering false ideals to people who believe their lies

Ill thoughts of hypocrisies being conjured up
By magicians who hide truth through tactics
Speaking down on poets like they are not worthy

Cause to make us outcasts would mean to mute our spirits
Throwing smoke and mirrors so the blind can't see nor hear
Our elixir being thrown through words so sublime- U must drink

Still they wonder why they walk around like lost sheep in the meadows
Letting wolfs in sheep's clothing sharp suits and pearl white teeth
Tell them what they want you to know not realizing UR mind been snowed

Assimilation was not the best medicine for their poisonous decrees
From making us 3/5th of a man to putting chicken pox in a papoose crib
All the way down to They got to have WMD's holed up and stored

Lost in perception that all is good, but it's not!
Still looking for leaders with no bull shit philosophies
Can't you see politicians turned our government into a mockery

No child left behind, the biggest joke to kill our future plans
Maybe they haven't been to our communities- our Hood Country Club
Where mayhem and ignorance forces us to become street smart

Still children in our neighborhoods don't have the educational tools
That children of the suburbs have to fulfill a life beyond desolation
I speak of computers, a full library to make research accessible

Maybe they just don't care or maybe they just don't understand
Saying fuck them who are they anyways
Our children be the future, growing up with street mentalities

These mentalities hold your greatest competition

For they are learning survival and pride despite the issues
Cause' adversity from the Pharisees has always made our generations stronger.

Yo, fuck that, no more Mr. Nice guy tap dancing over landmines
Time to stand up fight for what's right or lose all we died for
Yet we still paying for our education from a system bred to kill us

Ghetto philosophies so much hypocrisies from green back paid leaders
Are we that blind that we can't see his Mercedes is not righteous
Uncle Sam is taking us for everything and we owe him NOTHIN'

We blind folded like owls during daylight
You do the math We Shall Overcome is a lost pastime
Holding hands with politicians who is the NME really killing?[1]

She Dances… She Drums…

A child so meek and mild-
Yet, bearing the soul of an Ancestor.
The Revolution starts in the glimmer
of a child's eye

An old soul in such a body...

She dances to the drums from afar embedded in her conscious...

Restless in the night you can hear the melodies she creates in the wind with the sway of her hips and the move of her limbs...

Some say she is too young to move as the spirits do...

I say let her be to BE all that manifests and moves her groove so smooth...

From R&B to the ancient talking drums she moves...

SO much wiser is the soul encased in such a small body...

And when her physical tires she moves to create the elixir of intellect and past recollections with her drum...

So often I have sat back watching her grow with every rhythm she sends to the heavens...

Blistered hands... cuts in skin....As if offering her very flesh as a sacrifice to the ancestors who have blessed this little one...

She captures your own beating heart to be in unison with her majestic sounds...

Who is she you may ask...

This angelic blessing with gifts unimaginable...

Why she is a part of me...She is the fruits of my labor...

Quite beautiful she is merely 10...
She is Ashanti.

Revolution-
Bastard of Freedumb and Death

I can't get Freedumb
Death is not an option
I don't know how to die
What is left

The Bastard child of the unholy Union

Birthed in Freedumb miles away from Liberation
Death in my soul yet strong for Confrontation

What is the existence the poison of hour
A small lie so big it crushes our power

Underground papers and online sites
What is being achieved but stupid fights

Hidden agendas and drama abound
Can't get us together this time around

Fear of waking up to the front headlines
REVOLUTION is dead-we forgot our Ancestral Lines

We are the Bastards for refusing Assimilation...
Ostracized for defying Integration

We are resistant to the Master's Plans for Degradation
Refusing to drink from the cup of Colonization

Love is a memory and best left to the weak
Refusing for others to tell us when and where to speak

Kissing the thought of true peace aside
We pick up our pens weapons of our Pride

Revolution...

Back Against the Wall

> Through unwilling force the most peaceful in our struggle
> for liberation are faced with the fact sometimes
> we must truly live by the motto of Bro. Malcolm-
> "By Any Means Necessary"

It doesn't happen till the time is ripe.

When the REAL is revealed and your blessed lips

Are forced by the cosmos to utter in speech

Words refused by your womb to give birth before

Until through force of existence parlaying around you

"Fukk It", is born into your material manifestation

Then it becomes a warm blanket haters try to take from you

And you as the NEW Prophet they trying to put to death

Telling the back biters it is a NEW dawn and the old

Will get crushed by the harsh yet simplistic Proverbs of the Chosen

And as family and so-called friends tell you to stop cursing

You exclaim it is a BLESSED phrase the Ancestors have used since time-

When Xtian God looked at the Xtian Satan and said FUKK IT- Get out my house

Moses told his pharaoh brother FUKK this- Let MY People go

Pharaoh told Moses Fukk IT brother take them all

Thieves in the Temple- Money changers abound in HIS father's house

FUKK It was all that was said as the Son threw them out

Ancestral Mothers with newborns in hand refusing shackles

FUKK IT was the cry as they jumped ship to defy existence

Saying Fukk It all the way to Birmingham as evil in hoods

Tried to take our rights away- with every dog's bite

Can't stand Osama or Bush but with each test and trial

I am starting to love the way they proclaim Fukk It!

The dumb hoops my pen is being forced through

Turning my vowels dipped in tears into Terrorist threats

Got my mental forming WMD verses for all to behold

Training my Quill to strap a bomb PIECE to me

Call me an Insurgent- cause I refuse to be

A weak Infiltrator- I am up in your Nightmares

Simply I am every non-western culture- you can't get rid of me

Like Orishas' speech through the Middle Passage

I still have my power and Lyrical tone

Whether they in HOODS or from the HOOD

Testing my nerves I promise the Fakers and Shakers

Have given me a stronger voice to say

FUKK IT too!

When My Back Is Against the Wall

Revolutionary Mother

See, I was not built to have ladies in pink dresses

I was trained to turn around and create MORE soldiers.

I hate painting toe nails and giggling about boys or prom dates

I can't give advice on if a boy pull my hair type mess what it mean

Me and my girls don't have ladies day outs at Korean nail stores

We have lessons on ancient speech

I can train them to strip and clean a gun

The best herbs to heal a wound

I don't have time to see if the purse match the shoes

Who cares when before or after Labor Day we wear white again

We wear white year round to ask the Ancestors to wash away the blood

That we may have to spill by DEEDS or the BLOOD in my Pen

All that mindless numbing interaction makes my spirit ill

My man has complete faith in me if he ever goes down

His Wombman Child will learn arts of Intellectual War

The only love is the rest taken from the FIGHT of regaining Self

I teach the BEST camouflage techniques for different atmospheres

Which berries are bitter to taste and others that will sustain

How to follow trails and trap an NME in their pattern of speech

I do not teach integration or assimilation

I educate on stealth infiltration

I allow the Xbox and GameCube to be military tools

The latest combat simulation tracking and sniper

See, a Mother like me knows the hour

That the sands in the hourglass are slipping fast

So, excuse me if they hear a little cuss in my vernacular

If my tone is harsh at times it is to SNAP them out the clouds

Back in the trenches of the Daily grind to become Responsible for Self

So, I don't have time for dresses, slips or barrettes..

A Revolutionary Mother is what I was trained to be...

It is what I do best...

Vows For

The Revolution

Nothing is more sacred than two people equally yoked in all things. Two conscious minds melding a life together MUST be what the Creator intended for us in this day and time. May all the seeds planted in this union be blessed!

Will you birth my seed?

I will birth the seed of Truth to develop into the Zion of righteousness and world-shattering mindsets. I will couple with your soul to conceive generations of promise and dignity. I will labor your seed and cultivate the truth from the womb to dispel the future lies to stroke his ears and blind his eyes.

Will you die for me?

I will die to the light of ignorance and injustice. I will die to the belief my body is my own to corrupt at will. My tongue will die before ever speaking in opposition to the magnificence in you. I will die to the thoughts of self-indulgence and individualism. I will die to my last breathe charging the enemy with the slaughter of millions for them to obtain the Amerikkkan Dream.

Will you kill for me?

I will kill the seed of distrust and division between our brother and sisters. I will eradicate the wicked propaganda of the enemy which poisons our people daily to surrender to their will. I will gladly kill the miss-education forced to our children in miss-managed forgotten schools. I will kill the insecurity in your heart with my flow and encourage the warrior in you.

Will you live for me?

I will live to be by your side and alleviate the pains of this struggle. I will live to the hope of peace and comfort we will create in our Spoken Wordz. I will live in the silhouette of you to shine my radiance that will always carry you home. I will live to shield the Birthright given us through the blood of our ancestors from Slave Ship Jesus to Malcolm's last tears.

Vision-
Destruction in Liberation

The dust clears and we are beyond free...
Liberation is held in our hands do u feel me?
Eternity saved from a life of little white lies...
what will u do when this time flies?

To whom much is given much is required...
What is the plan to renew now they fired?
We have no government plan contingency
All we know is social activity...

So, shut up trying to step to me about baby we gonna have us a revolution!
Wake up and educate me on the aftermath affects and the New World execution...

Of our glorious future after the blood sweat and tears...
Tell me our future generations should not have these fears...

Tell me is there black dudes holed up with plans for a New Constitution?
Just like the white forefathers who set forth slavery as an American Institution...

Soothe my earth shattering visions of their generations laughing as we stumble...
What good is the Creator passing us the ball is all we gonna do is fumble?

What GOD would give us what we seek- with the lies we live...
All we do is seek individualism and have forgotten how to give...

Tell me our *wombman will be protected...*
Or will you turn your back in Crystal and Moet celebration leave us to be abducted...

Will we win the war just to destroy our very souls in lust and sin..
Will God do what HE has done in the past to make us start over again...

Why am I seeking to give life to Eternity?
How can I when our Liberation does not promise security?

Scribble Your Mind

The pen is mightier than the sword has been said since ink hit parchment.
As writers and Spoken Word Artists we prove this in the struggle everyday

I know it will take more than a second or two

But I have waited lifetimes for you to

Scribble Your Mind

Etch out the details of our New world

Say let there be darkness with your pen

Watch the flowers rebloom and amoebas become US

As we righteously become perfectly born again!

I want to sit and watch your intellect spill

Spill new directions and mindsets for our people

Make me high off the fumes of the eraser as you realize

Your mistakes and heat up the paper for correction

Allow my hips to dance in rhythm to the smooth

Scratching jazz coming from pen hitting' pad

See, it was not that hard to allow your mind

To discard OLD and emblazon NEW on tablets

Our life long lessons for the Promised Land

We look for Salvation where birds fly

Forgetting all our treasures are locked inside...

But you hold the KEY- Cause in your PEN

Holds OUR Destiny

Damn- Just Standing

I will not just stand....
when I have done all I can...

I will seek out those of us
who are ready to stop standing
and dig!!
Dig deep trenches and wait for
the whites of their
eyes
Dig spiritual trenches and be armed
with our ancestral
strength...

I will not just stand...
when I have done all I can...

I will train up the next generation
to take us
forward!
Train my mind and soul to
not endure them
anymore
I will train those willing
in the art of power
and pride...

I will not just stand...
when I have done all I can...

I will shake off the haters and
the egos of those around me
Shake off the mind control that
is trying to be fed to me
I will shake the mindsets of the dead
Until they awaken to the NME's plans...

This new age spiritual concept of standing and waiting is so we can be immobile while
they are progressing. Get off your knees and dust off the dirt!

Back to Eden

I got something inside me for you.
Memories of past lives and failed revolutions. We have to carry the pains of this existence out of this realm knowing failure is no option this time around.

How can I course through this time and space without fulfilling the destiny of reversing the ignorant mentalities put on us since creation?
The lie of no Eden forevermore shall be reversed.

Rims blinding and babies crying from the spinning blades of hunger pains... Rise my King...Your people are here I can't do this alone.

Harriet may have brought bodies Up North but the soul was rooted in Deep South and destined to die there. Angela Davis can speak. Maya can write with the blood of the Ancients. Nature can create the torrents to break the levees and try to wake my people up. Bush doesn't care about you!!!

Only your command can bend the trickster and make HIM protect the house that YOU built. Rise My Black man cause w/o your guidance ordained by the Creator that all this is yours to reign over... We are only walking death.

Walking wombs bearing dead babies to walk and bling in death. Gold grills blood dripped diamonds from ears Saggin' pants which in the mirror spells Niggas... (Think about it). Lies of quick money and schemes gone wrong- piling and dying in the correctional facilities to come out walking fiercer than Ms. Jay and any Next Top Model.

Walking wombs bringing forth newborn Beyonce getting' Bootylicious and knowing sex before sex knows her own mind. Entranced in Video hoes and pushed into the reality of another woman's touch with the smoke of one blunt and one too many failed relationships.

Time out for our cartoonist love affairs where we spout righteous rhetoric.
Feeding orgies and three ways instead of the true Collective Family.
I respect you... You respect me and we all just live and let the children be.
Let them be raised in the consciousness of our ancestors.

To know Malcolm died in the glory all men should desire. Queen Nzingha was no bytch... That Shaka Zulu was destroyed for he possessed the knowledge of the Orishas. I get lost in the rhythmic methodic destruction of the Aboriginal People of every land they ever spread their lies to.

Action is required or we will pass from this realm yet again poisoning a generation of Indigo Blue- the cosmic aura of the elevated consciousness- we bear fruit and drop into this life to forget their destiny given and granted by the Most High.
Allowing them to develop the slave mentality of the evil intended ones.

  I got something inside me for you.
Memories of past lives and failed revolutions. We have to carry the pains of this existence out of this realm knowing failure is no option this time around.

How can I course through this time and space without fulfilling the destiny of reversing the ignorant mentalities put on us since creation?
The lie of no Eden forevermore shall be reversed.

Birthed In Lines

We are a generation conceived and birthed through society's lines- Welfare lines-
government cheese lines- food stamp lines- slave ship lines- whipping post lines-
unemployment lines- Yeah, we forgot about the ancestral lines of dignity and pride.

We dismiss the lines of trails and tears carved through the South to find North, and the
astronomical lines of the pyramids. We created the force of lines- now lines are our
prison. Grocery store lines for food unfit even for the filthiest pig- movie lines devouring
our paychecks we worked for to see an action hero that is nothing like us. When the real
Mission Impossible is to break away from the lines.

 Lines- Lines how did we get trapped in public school lines- lines zoning our kids with
outdated books with our line of history starting and stopping with slavery. Emergency
room lines-Death Row Lines- divorce court lines- lines of censorship through our words
of freedom and equality.

We are a generation conceived and birthed through society's lines- Welfare lines-
government cheese lines- food stamp lines- slave ship lines- whipping post lines-
unemployment lines- Yeah, we forgot about the ancestral lines of dignity and pride.

Colored only lines- Post reconstruction Soup Lines- XXX movie theatre lines- Lies of
corruption to entice the senses to keep us in these lines of treachery and deceit. Draft
Lines many black men were forced to cross- Medicaid lines where they push sterilization
onto our young daughters-

Aids medication lines- illiteracy lines- paternity test lines because society tells us we are
free to be immoral and dress to impress. Lines in a diamond dipped in blood from mother
Africa. Yeah many of you bleeding lines now from your hands and ears blood drenched
grills blinding in the face of your people and the wrath of The Creator.

We are a generation conceived and birthed through society's lines- Welfare lines-
government cheese lines- food stamp lines- slave ship lines- whipping post lines-
unemployment lines- Yeah, we forgot about the ancestral lines of dignity and pride.

The Journey Ends...

Jah's Creation

"My family and my life motivate me." Born October 20th 1974 she has resided in Houston Texas all her life. She often reflects on her poetry style as Cultural.

"I say I am a Cultural poet because as a people we are the Revolution, we are Love and we are Faith."

She embarked on her writing journey at the age of 10. Her pen name is Jah's Creation. Simply stated it means One Created by God.

"I speak on our past because I was close to my great-grandparents/grand-parents. I did not live through most of what our people went through but I had Great Elders who were mindful in not letting us forget."

"I grew up around African tradionalist and Rastafarians since I was 15. So, I knew GOD as Jah and Oludumare right after I knew Allah and Jesus. I am humbled to say I am diverse in our people and traditions."

"I point out the issues to start a dialogue on solutions. I don't have all the answers but I hope my works are one avenue to progress."

Currently, Jah's is working on a CD with "Da'God Supreme" fana. It will consist of new material and also prose from the book.

"Everything I write is from personal experience. Every love piece and so-called Militant piece is from my heart. To share that part of me with the world; I hope makes a positive impact on someone's life."

"Truly this legacy is for my children."

Acknowledgements

1. "Bound 2 U" and "Stolen Truth"- Collaboration with Defiant Sun contact info:
   www.cdbaby.com/defiantsun
   www.myspace.com/defiantson

2. "Ancient Devotions"- Orisa in Yoruba/Ifa religiosity.

3. Revolution Intro Page- Haiku "Jah's Creation" used with permission by:
   Perditionslovechild http://www.myspace.com/MsDestinie (R.I.P.- sister)

Cover Page Design- *Sahara Wisdom*

I want to thank Supreme for never allowing me to be stagnate. Your determination to ensure Amir and Aadhira's mommy never stayed in self pity and doubt is why I am re-releasing this book and continuing on my writing journey.

MAJOR love must go to my family of BPC (www.theblackpoetrycafe.com) for fine tuning and sending my PEN and thoughts through the FIRE.

My great grandfather for the stories he told me as a child. The life he lived in the South with my Creole grandmother. Yes, poppy I have passed along those stories to my kids. I have to thank my grandmother and my Aunt for raising the child in me.

Also, Ayo Muhammad (my spiritual mother), Nzinga and Hassein you accepted and loved me in The Creator's name of Allah.

Thanks, to my father, Reginal Hill, for raising me. You taught me survival despite my surroundings. A gift I can never pay back.

I can't miss my brothers and my baby sister. YES Carmen Amelia, you are my lil' devil/angel always. Michael you still give me headaches but that is what big brothers are for. Jason I love you immensely. You will always have a place in my heart and family. We are all so different yet I am proud to be a part of each and every one of you. You inspire me.

Last, but not least, A'Kwanzaa Unique, Ajee' Eboni, Ashanti Essence and Lizzy Lenich. My young ladies, grown women.. my children. Without you as my anchors I would not be here. I love you my beautiful daughters.

www.ingramcontent.com/pod-product-compliance
Lightning Source LLC
Chambersburg PA
CBHW022348040426
42449CB00006B/774